Hearts Across the Heavens

In the silence of the night,
Two souls connect in flight.
Stars whisper all their dreams,
In celestial silver streams.

Across the darkened skies,
Love's glow softly lies.
Guiding each step they take,
Through the paths that they make.

With every twinkling light,
Hearts entwine, shining bright.
Distance melts like the snow,
As the universe starts to glow.

Original title:
The Constellation of Connection

Copyright © 2024 Swan Charm
All rights reserved.

Author: Sara Säde
ISBN HARDBACK: 978-9916-86-743-3
ISBN PAPERBACK: 978-9916-86-744-0
ISBN EBOOK: 978-9916-86-745-7

Celestial Bridges

Through the void, they build a way,
Bridges made of stars that sway.
Galaxies pulsating with grace,
Uniting worlds in a warm embrace.

Dreamers navigate the night,
With hearts set on the flight.
Guided by a distant spark,
Finding joy within the dark.

Every heartbeat sings a tune,
Underneath the watchful moon.
Threads of light, a tapestry,
Woven in shared harmony.

Navigating the Night Sky

With maps of stars, they roam afar,
Charting courses by each star.
Every shimmer tells a tale,
As they set their sights to sail.

Guided by the constellations,
Finding hope in hesitations.
Whispers of the cosmic flow,
Light the path that they will go.

In this vast and endless sea,
They discover unity.
Holding fast to dreams so high,
Together, they will fly.

Binding Light

In the heart of the night,
Two beings hold their light.
With dreams intertwined, they soar,
Through the realms of evermore.

Casting shadows far behind,
They seek the truth that's blind.
Chasing whispers on the breeze,
With each flickering release.

Through the vast and endless space,
They find warmth in every place.
Binding light, their spirits rise,
Forever under starlit skies.

Celestial Ties

In the night, our dreams ignite,
Holding hands, we chase the light.
Stars align as whispers soar,
In this dance, we long for more.

Galaxies twinkle, hearts entwined,
In this universe, love defined.
With every pulse, a secret shared,
In cosmic silence, we're declared.

Through the void, our voices blend,
Boundless journeys, never end.
Together we traverse the skies,
Creating truths in starry sighs.

Threads Among Stars

Woven through the fabric bright,
Threads of silver, pure delight.
Each constellation tells a tale,
Of love that braves the cosmic gale.

From distant realms, we pull the seams,
Stitching fate with shared dreams.
Through the dark, a tapestry,
Binding souls in mystery.

Every nebula, a gentle nudge,
In this space, we will not budge.
Threads of stardust dashed in time,
Woven patterns, so sublime.

Weaving Starlit Bonds

In twilight's glow, our hearts align,
We weave through shadows, ever thine.
With each spark, a promise grows,
In starlit nights, affection flows.

Together gliding, soul in flight,
A tapestry bathed in moonlight.
Kisses woven in the dark,
Eternal echoes, love's sweet spark.

The cosmos sings our silent tune,
Beneath the watchful eyes of moon.
Hand in hand, we craft the light,
In woven bonds, forever bright.

Celestial Conversations

Stars converse in whispers low,
Each twinkle holds a story's glow.
In the silence, secrets shared,
Cosmic thoughts that both have bared.

Across the void, we trade our hopes,
In galactic folds, love elopes.
The night becomes a sacred space,
Where every glance, a warm embrace.

From celestial shores, we find our way,
Guided by the light of day.
In conversations through the night,
We build a world with pure insight.

The Universe Speaks in Connections

In silence, stars collide,
Linking hearts side by side.
Glistening in the night,
Whispers of love take flight.

Galaxies dance afar,
Binding us like a star.
Threads of fate intertwined,
In the cosmos, we find.

Atoms hum a sweet tune,
Under the watchful moon.
Every heartbeat a spark,
Lighting our way through dark.

Across this vast expanse,
We share a timeless dance.
A bond that won't be broken,
In each word softly spoken.

Through constellations bright,
We embrace the cosmic light.
Together we will dream,
In the universe's gleam.

Starry Threads of Affection

Beneath the velvet sky,
We find love's gentle sigh.
Stars twinkle, softly sway,
Binding us in their play.

The moon, a guardian's gaze,
Guiding us through the haze.
Every star a promise made,
In the night, our hearts laid.

Woven in cosmic streams,
Our laughter fuels the dreams.
Each moment stitched with grace,
In this celestial space.

As comets blaze and glide,
Feel the warmth deep inside.
With every wish we make,
Starry threads never break.

Bound by invisible ties,
We watch the world arise.
In the universe's embrace,
Love finds its destined place.

Cosmic Reflections of Relationship

In mirrors of the night,
Love reflects purest light.
Planets spin, intertwined,
Harmony we shall find.

Shooting stars cascade down,
Wearing joy like a crown.
Echoes of laughter bloom,
Chasing away the gloom.

Universes collide,
In each other's hearts, confide.
Whispers of dreams, they soar,
In this space we adore.

Galactic love unfolds,
In stories yet untold.
With every glance we share,
We float on cosmic air.

Our journey never ends,
In this dance, love transcends.
Through the endless expanse,
We hold a sacred chance.

Weaving Light in the Darkness

In shadows, we find light,
Together, hearts take flight.
Woven dreams, soft as night,
Illuminate with delight.

Through trials, we stand strong,
In each other's arms, belong.
Stars align, paths divine,
Creating moments fine.

Thread by thread, we create,
A tapestry of fate.
Love threads like golden rays,
Guiding us through our days.

In the depths, we still shine,
With hope as our design.
We build a world so bright,
Weaving love in the night.

As darkness comes to fade,
In the magic we've made,
Light will always arise,
In the love that never dies.

Infinite Night's Promise

In the silence of the night, we soar,
Promises whispered, forevermore.
Stars align in a shimmering dance,
Echoes of fate in every glance.

Moonlight wraps us in its embrace,
Time stands still in this sacred space.
Dreams unfold like petals in bloom,
Infinite night dispels all gloom.

Together we chase what's yet to find,
Bound by the rhythms of heart and mind.
In shadows cast by the cosmic tide,
Infinite whispers, our souls abide.

Heartstrings in the Milky Way

Underneath the vast tapestry,
Heartstrings hum a sweet melody.
Galaxies twirl in a graceful flight,
Binding our souls through endless night.

Constellations spark in the dark,
Each one tells tales, leaving a mark.
Together we drift, hand in hand,
Within this realm, forever we stand.

As comets blaze with fiery trails,
Love's journey triumphs, never fails.
In the Milky Way, our hearts entwine,
A cosmic dance, eternally divine.

Embraced by Stardust

Beneath the glow of distant suns,
In stardust dreams, our story runs.
Galactic winds whisper our names,
In this embrace, nothing remains the same.

Floating softly in the night air,
Every heartbeat whispers, 'You're my care.'
Nebulas shimmer with colors bright,
Wrapped in warmth of cosmic light.

Each moment lingers, a gentle kiss,
In the tapestry of cosmic bliss.
Embraced by stardust, we are whole,
Infinite wonders, one shared soul.

Celestial Compass

Guided by the stars' gentle glow,
A celestial compass, helping us grow.
Through the night's canvas, we roam,
Finding our way, forever our home.

Each spark of light, a destiny's call,
In the universe vast, we can't help but fall.
With every heartbeat, the cosmos sings,
A map of love that the nighttime brings.

Together we navigate this grand design,
Through cosmic seas where our hearts align.
In twilight's embrace, hand in hand,
With the celestial compass, forever we stand.

Whispers in the Cosmos

Stars glimmer, secrets bright,
Echoes of a silent night.
Galaxies in gentle sway,
Whispers of the dreams that play.

Comets dance with fleeting grace,
Across the vast, eternal space.
Each twinkling, a soft sigh,
As worlds beyond us drift and fly.

Nebulas in colors bold,
Stories waiting to be told.
In shadows deep, new suns ignite,
A symphony of cosmic light.

Time and distance intertwine,
In the void where stars align.
With every breath, we find our way,
In whispers that the cosmos say.

Fleeting moments, captured clear,
In the vastness, we draw near.
Listening to the night's soft tune,
Finding fate beneath the moon.

Interwoven Destinies

Threads of fate, we weave and spin,
In every loss, a chance to win.
Paths that cross and paths that part,
Every bond, a work of art.

Stories written in the stars,
Lives entwined, despite the scars.
With every choice, the pattern grows,
In unison, our journey flows.

Through laughter shared, through tears we shed,
Every step, a path we tread.
In the tapestry of time so wide,
Together still, we move and bide.

Fates like rivers, twist and turn,
In their flow, our passions burn.
Embraced by grace, we walk anew,
With every thread, a different view.

In the dance of life, we find the rhyme,
Our destinies hold hands through time.
With every heartbeat, we define,
The beauty of this grand design.

Threads of Light

Silken strands of dawn's first glow,
In quiet corners, soft and slow.
Weaving dreams with every beam,
Threads of light, a waking dream.

Each moment shines, a flickered spark,
Guiding footsteps through the dark.
With every thread, a story told,
In the warmth, we find our gold.

Rays of sun, like whispers sweet,
Kissing earth with gentle heat.
In the morning's tender embrace,
Threads of light weave time and space.

Through shadows cast, they break away,
Leading hearts to brighter day.
In every crack, a glimmer's might,
Hope is born from threads of light.

As day unfolds and night descends,
The tapestry of life transcends.
In every thread, a chance to start,
Weaving love, in every heart.

Celestial Harmonies

In the stillness of the night,
Celestial bodies gleam so bright.
Tuning forks of starry sound,
Harmony in space is found.

The moon hums a tranquil song,
As planets dance, a rhythmic throng.
Galaxies in perfect time,
Creating beauty, pure and prime.

In every note, a wish takes flight,
Echoing through the endless night.
With cosmic chords that lift the soul,
In this vastness, we find our role.

Stars collide and fusion starts,
Filling voids with vibrant arts.
In symphony, we hear the pulse,
Of nature's song, a grand impulse.

Together in this cosmic play,
We dance to rhythms night and day.
In harmony, let spirits soar,
Celestial music evermore.

Cosmic Intimacies

In the quiet night sky,
Whispers of dreams unfold.
Galaxies dance in rhythm,
Secrets in stardust told.

Hearts beat with the cosmos,
Boundless, yet so near.
Each twinkle tells a story,
Of love that conquers fear.

Nebulas paint the heavens,
A canvas rich and vast.
Every spark a promise,
Of shadows from the past.

Time weaves through the darkness,
A tapestry of light.
Souls mingle in the silence,
In the depth of night.

Together, we are stardust,
In this endless embrace.
Cosmic intimacies bloom,
In the void of space.

Starlight's Legacy

Beneath the endless heavens,
Where light begins to fade,
The whispers of the ancients,
In every star conveyed.

Echoes through the ages,
Stories born from fire.
Legacies of starlight,
Inspire and inspire.

Each constellation gleams,
With history untold.
A map of hidden journeys,
Of hearts both brave and bold.

Legends thread the twilight,
With silver in their veins.
In the arms of darkness,
Life's wisdom still remains.

A night of endless wonder,
With dreams that intertwine.
Starlight's legacy shines bright,
In the grand divine.

Stars Aligned in Harmony

In the chorus of the night,
Stars intertwine and sway.
Fragrant breaths of wonder,
Guide the heart's own way.

Whirling in the cosmos,
A dance both soft and true.
Galaxies unite,
In the moments shared by few.

Each spark a point of unity,
In the vast expanse of dark.
Creating bonds of starlight,
With destiny's bright mark.

Cradled in the silence,
Where dreams begin to hum.
The universe sings gently,
To the beat of all that's come.

Stars aligned in harmony,
In a celestial embrace.
Together, we are stardust,
In time and space.

Threads of Celestial Bonding

Across the velvet canvas,
Threads of light connect.
Invisible but strong,
In every soul, reflect.

Whispers of the cosmos,
Entwined with tender care.
Each thread a gentle moment,
In the silent air.

Bound by starlit dreams,
In a dance that feels so right.
Celestial bonding flows,
Through the tapestry of night.

With each heartbeat echoing,
In sync with lunar dreams.
The universe unravels,
In the melody it seems.

Threads of cosmic weaving,
With stories all their own.
In the vastness of creation,
Together, we have grown.

Radiant Trails of Affinity

Beneath the stars that softly gleam,
Connections form like a shared dream.
Each heart a beacon, bright and bold,
Unfolding tales that need be told.

Whispers dance on the evening air,
Binding souls with a gentle care.
In laughter light, in silence deep,
These radiant trails our hearts will keep.

From fleeting glances to warm embrace,
We find our paths, we carve our space.
With every moment that passes by,
Affinity blooms, reaching high.

Through winding roads, we wander free,
Together, we shape our destiny.
In every heartbeat, a spark ignites,
Leading us through the starry nights.

In every story, we find our role,
In sacred bonds that heal the soul.
Through radiant trails, we intertwine,
Forever bound, your heart and mine.

The Sky's Secrets of Unity

The sky unfolds in hues so bright,
A tapestry of day and night.
Together we gaze, lost in wonder,
Revealing secrets like rolling thunder.

Clouds drift softly, a gentle sail,
In unity's song, we share the tale.
Each star a link in our shared fate,
Inviting us to celebrate.

In twilight's glow, shadows unite,
Guiding us home through the quiet night.
Hand in hand, we journey far,
Under the watch of a familiar star.

The moon whispers softly, casting light,
On dreams we weave in the silent night.
Through every trial, we stand together,
Bound by threads of a timeless tether.

As constellations shift and sway,
We find our strength in love's display.
The sky reveals its secrets vast,
In unity's embrace, we'll hold steadfast.

Tracing Patterns of Togetherness

In the fabric of life, threads entwine,
Weaving patterns, yours and mine.
Every moment, a stitch we make,
In the quilt of dreams, for love's sake.

Like rivers flowing, side by side,
Our paths converge, no need to hide.
In every smile, in every sigh,
Together we reach for the boundless sky.

Through seasons changing, hand in hand,
We navigate this sacred land.
Each laugh a thread, each tear a seam,
Tracing patterns, living the dream.

In the tapestry of time we trust,
United in faith, in hope we must.
With every heartbeat, a rhythm strong,
Together, we sing our song.

As we journey forth, we'll not forget,
The patterns of love that we beget.
In every story we come to see,
Together we'll write our destiny.

Fated Connections in the Milky Way

Stars align in cosmic dance,
Whispers of fate in every glance.
Galaxies spin, we find our place,
In the vastness, a warm embrace.

Hearts entwined like nebulae bright,
Guided softly by starlit light.
In this universe, we converge,
On a path where dreams emerge.

With every pulse, our spirits soar,
In the silence, we hear the roar.
Time stands still, eclipsing the night,
Bound together, our minds take flight.

Through black holes, we boldly glide,
In the dance of stars, we confide.
Every heartbeat echoes the sway,
Of fated connections in the Milky Way.

Celestial Bonds: Invisible Yet Strong

Through the ether, unseen threads weave,
Silent promises that never deceive.
Each heartbeat a whisper, each glance a guide,
In celestial wonders, our hopes abide.

Invisible bonds hold us in place,
Through cosmic storms, we find our grace.
Galactic echoes remind us we're one,
Under the watch of the radiant sun.

Detours may come, yet we never part,
Your light is a map, a compass for the heart.
In the tapestry of stars, we find our way,
Celestial love, forever will stay.

With every spark, our souls align,
In the universe, a sacred sign.
Invisible yet strong, our love is true,
Filaments of stardust guiding me to you.

Across the Sky, Threads of Us

Across the sky, our stories blend,
In the twilight haze, our dreams extend.
Under the blanket of the endless night,
Stars illuminate the path so bright.

In every constellation, a laughter shared,
Memories glowing, moments declared.
A cosmic quilt of hopes, we create,
Entwined like roots, in love, we await.

Shooting stars carry wishes near,
In the silence, your voice I hear.
Feel the rhythm of our hearts, so close,
Threads of us weave what we cherish most.

Celestial currents pull us tight,
Drawing strength through darkest nights.
Across the expanse, our desires flow,
In the vast unknown, together we grow.

Harmonious Whirls in Celestial Space

In the dance of galaxies, we glide,
Harmonious whirls, side by side.
With every spin, a note in time,
Echoes of love in stars that chime.

Planets orbit in perfect tune,
Under the gaze of the silver moon.
Astral melodies, sweet and clear,
In this symphony, I hold you near.

Vibrations drift on solar winds,
A timeless song where our journey begins.
In spiral arms, our spirits sway,
Found in rhythm, come what may.

From supernovae to gentle light,
Every moment feels just right.
Harmonious whirls, our hearts embrace,
In this wondrous, celestial space.

Echoes of Souls Across Time

Whispers of the past, silently they creep,
Through the corridors of time, secrets deep.
Each heartbeat a memory, vibrant and true,
Carried by the winds, like morning dew.

Fragments of laughter, echoes of tears,
Binding our spirits across distant years.
In the silence, we find the threads we weave,
Connecting our journeys, together we believe.

Footsteps of shadows, dancing in light,
Guiding us gently through the endless night.
In the tapestry of moments, rich and rare,
Our souls intertwine, a bond we share.

The river of time flows, steady and slow,
Carving out stories that forever glow.
In the echoes, we hear what words rarely say,
Our spirits united, come what may.

Through lives and ages, we carry the spark,
Illuminating paths, even in the dark.
Every heartbeat sings, a timeless refrain,
In the echoes of souls, love will remain.

Celestial Strings of Togetherness

Under the canopy of stars, we roam,
Galaxies whispering of our shared home.
Celestial strings pull our hearts, entwined,
In the vast universe, two souls aligned.

Twilight dances on the edge of night,
Reflecting the warmth of our shared light.
Each constellation tells a tale of old,
Of bonds unbroken, of stories bold.

In the space between breaths, we find our grace,
A melody soaring through timeless space.
Woven together, we sing as one,
Chasing the shadows, embracing the sun.

With every heartbeat, the universe spins,
Creating a rhythm where friendship begins.
A celestial chorus in harmony flows,
In the symphony of togetherness, love grows.

As stars collide in a glorious blaze,
Our spirits ignite in a cosmic phase.
Through the tapestry of life, hand in hand,
Together we journey, together we stand.

Light Years of Friendship

Across the cosmos, our laughter gleams,
A universe built from shared dreams.
Light years between us, yet close at heart,
In the fabric of time, we are never apart.

Traveling stardust on this endless quest,
Each moment together, a cherished guest.
Through trials and triumphs, we hold the line,
In the vast expanse, your soul shines with mine.

Celestial wonders in every glance,
In the dance of friendship, we take our chance.
With each passing day, we grow and learn,
In the heart's ignition, bright fires burn.

Linked by the stars that shimmer above,
We navigate worlds with the compass of love.
Together we soar through the cosmic tide,
In light years of friendship, forever we ride.

As constellations form beneath our gaze,
We celebrate life in countless ways.
For across every galaxy, near and far,
True friendship's light is our guiding star.

Galaxies Intertwined in Spirit

In the spiral dance of celestial spheres,
Our spirits entwine through laughter and tears.
Galaxies collide in a magnificent glow,
Creating a tapestry of love we bestow.

Across the cosmos, we travel as one,
Chasing the shadows, embracing the sun.
In the silence of night, hear our hearts call,
In this vast universe, we rise and we fall.

With each heartbeat, the stars play their tune,
A symphony woven beneath the pale moon.
In the essence of friendship, we find our way,
Guided by starlight each night and each day.

Threads of existence connect us in grace,
Moments shared in this infinite space.
Through the dance of galaxies, we understand,
In the spirit of love, forever we stand.

As we drift through the cosmos, hand in hand,
In the beauty of friendship, we make our stand.
Eternally linked, wherever we go,
Galaxies intertwined, our spirits in flow.

Cosmic Threads of Unity

In the vastness of night, we find our place,
Threads of light weaving through time and space.
Stars glimmer softly, a gentle embrace,
Connected in silence, we share this grace.

Whispers of stardust dance on the breeze,
Binding our hearts like the rustling leaves.
In the cosmic web, where all souls tease,
Unity blooms, as the spirit believes.

Galaxies swirl in a wondrous ballet,
Each twinkle a promise, a new dawn's play.
Together we journey, come what may,
In the tapestry of life, we find our way.

Harmony echoes in every bright spark,
Illuminating paths through the endless dark.
With each step together, we leave our mark,
Cosmic threads connecting, igniting a spark.

As the universe sings of our shared quest,
We find in each heartbeat a timeless rest.
In the dance of the cosmos, we are blessed,
In unity's arms, we are ever compressed.

Harmonies Beyond the Horizon

Beyond the horizon, where dreams take flight,
   Melodies linger in the soft twilight.
  Every note woven with pure delight,
  Harmonies echo, the world feels right.

Waves of the ocean, a symphonic embrace,
    Nature's rhythm, in perfect grace.
  Together we sway, in this sacred space,
  Each heartbeat aligning, a shared pace.

In the whispering winds, our voices align,
  Creating a chorus that transcends the line.
  Bound by the music, the stars intertwine,
Under the night sky, our souls brightly shine.

The colors of sunset in vibrant display,
  Chords of our laughter in a dazzling array.
  As we share this moment, come what may,
  Together we journey, our spirits will play.

In the silence of night, our hearts will sing,
  The harmonies found in each little thing.
  Beyond the horizon, as timeless we cling,
    In unity's song, our souls take wing.

Constellations of Togetherness

In the tapestry of night, constellations glow,
Each star a story, together we know.
Guided by light, through the shadows we go,
In the depths of darkness, our spirits will grow.

We map our journey through the cosmic seas,
Bound by the wonders carried on the breeze.
Each glimmer a promise, a simple tease,
In the arms of togetherness, we find ease.

From distant worlds, we hear the call,
In unity's grace, we will never fall.
Together we rise, through the rise and squall,
Constellations beckon, inviting us all.

The universe whispers wisdom and cheer,
In every heartbeat, our love draws near.
With compassion and kindness, we'll persevere,
Creating connections that flourish here.

Beneath the splendor of the infinite night,
We weave our stories, a tapestry bright.
In constellations, we draw our true sight,
Together forever, we shine with delight.

A Galaxy of Understanding

In the expanse of stars, we seek to find,
A galaxy of thoughts, intertwined.
With open hearts, we leave fear behind,
Exploring the depths of the human mind.

Through nebulae bright, our spirits explore,
Each question a portal, opening doors.
In dialogue softly, our wisdom soars,
Creating a bridge, love ever restores.

Across cosmic borders, we share our grace,
Finding reflections in every face.
In the silence of knowing, we find our place,
A galaxy where kindness will interlace.

Each moment a treasure, each smile a star,
Brightening pathways that stretch near and far.
In the heart of the cosmos, who we are,
Understanding blossoms, no limit, no bar.

As we journey together under the night,
We gather the wisdom, embrace the light.
In a galaxy spun from compassion's might,
United in purpose, we shine ever bright.

Orbiting Hearts

In the dance of night skies,
Two souls intertwine as one.
Their love spins like planets,
Orbiting, never to come undone.

A gentle pull of desire,
Gravity draws them near.
Through trials and time they wander,
Always finding their way here.

With whispers of the cosmos,
They share secrets of the stars.
In the quiet of the universe,
Their hearts beat, free of scars.

As constellations shift and sway,
They navigate through the unknown.
Hand in hand, they explore the night,
Together, they have grown.

In this celestial ballet,
Their love ignites the dark,
A flame that burns eternally,
A never-fading spark.

Lightyears of Affection

Across the vast expanse,
Love travels faster than light.
Every heartbeat a message,
In the silence of the night.

Through the void of empty space,
Yearning souls reach out wide.
Each touch a pulse of warmth,
A journey taken in stride.

In the glow of distant stars,
Their laughter fills the air.
Each moment an eternity,
A bond beyond compare.

With memories like stardust,
They weave dreams in the dark.
Lightyears of affection,
An ever-brightening mark.

Forever chasing shadowed paths,
Where love becomes their guide.
In the tapestry of the heavens,
Together, they forever glide.

Starborn Connections

From the heart of the universe,
They find a sacred thread.
Woven through the fabric,
Of dreams that lie ahead.

Like comets through the night,
They blaze a fiery trail.
Two starborn souls, entwined,
In a love that will not fail.

Each flicker, a promise made,
In the silence of the vast.
Their spirits soar in freedom,
Embraced by the endless cast.

Among the shimmering heavens,
Their laughter lights the way.
In the dance of celestial bodies,
Together they will stay.

Bound by invisible forces,
They journey without end.
In the constellation of their hearts,
Eternally, they'll mend.

Celestial Embrace

In the arms of the galaxy,
Two hearts find their place.
A tender, cosmic union,
Wrapped in a starry embrace.

With every breath of starlight,
They share whispers of dreams.
In the expanse of the ether,
Love flows like flowing streams.

The moon watches over them,
As they dance on the tide.
Each wave a soft caress,
In the world where they reside.

Through nebulas and shadows,
They chase the light of dawn.
With each pulse of the cosmos,
A new adventure is drawn.

In this celestial haven,
Their spirits rise and roam.
Together in the universe,
They've finally found their home.

Celestial Reflections

The stars whisper secrets soft,
In the velvet night they drift.
Mirrors of dreams, they shine aloft,
Guiding hearts with their gentle gift.

Planets dance in a cosmic waltz,
Orbiting tales of ages past.
In their glow, our troubles halt,
Moments of peace, forever cast.

Galaxies converge, collide with grace,
A tapestry woven, vast and bright.
Each twinkle tells a story's trace,
In the canvas of eternal night.

Comets blaze across the skies,
Trails of brilliance, fleeting and bold.
With every flash, a wish it flies,
In the cosmic ink, our fates are scrolled.

Beneath the stars, we rise, we fall,
In the celestial choir, we find our voice.
A universe grand, answering our call,
In the dance of light, we rejoice.

Embracing the Void

In the silence where shadows blend,
Chaos awaits with open arms.
The void beckons, a timeless friend,
Whispering secrets, weaving charms.

Embrace the darkness, let it mend,
The fractured light within your soul.
In absence of form, we transcend,
Finding freedom in the whole.

Stars are born from cosmic tears,
Yet in their birth, a void remains.
Through endless cycles, fate endears,
Out of emptiness, everything gains.

Fear not the blackness, for it's wise,
It holds the crux of life's design.
In every end, a new arise,
From the void, our spirits align.

Journey deep where silence dwells,
Beyond the known, let go, let be.
In the heart of the void, truth swells,
In its embrace, we find the key.

Stellar Kinship

Under a blanket of constellations,
We gather like dust in the night.
Each star a bond, a shared creation,
Together, we soar, bound by light.

Through cosmic winds and solar flare,
Our paths intersect, fates entwine.
In the vastness, we find our care,
In stellar kinship, we brightly shine.

Pulsars sing in rhythmic beats,
Echoing a love that never fades.
In their pulse, our journey repeats,
Through the galaxy, we dance in shades.

Nebulas paint our shared dreams,
Colorful whispers of joy and pain.
In the light, our essence beams,
Through the tears, our laughter reigns.

Together we navigate the skies,
On this celestial voyage, we thrive.
In every spark, a connection lies,
In stellar kinship, forever alive.

The Language of Light

In the dawn, the sun speaks clear,
Painting gold on the waking earth.
Every ray a message near,
Illuminating life since birth.

Moonbeams weave tales at dusk,
Softly shining on the serene.
In their glow, we find the musk,
Of dreams awakened, yet unseen.

Colors whisper in the breeze,
A symphony of sight and sound.
In every hue, a heart at ease,
In the spectrum, unity found.

Light travels far, with stories to share,
From quasar bursts to gentle glow.
In every blink, we sense the care,
Of cosmic wonders, sparking flow.

The dance of photons, a vibrant play,
In each flash, a world ignites.
Together we cherish every ray,
In the language of light, our spirits take flight.

Navigating by Shared Stars

In the night, we find our way,
Stars twinkle in a cosmic ballet.
With every step, our paths align,
Guided by light, your hand in mine.

Whispers echo in the dark,
Wishing on wishes, igniting a spark.
Together we sail on dreams so bright,
Navigating through the velvet night.

Each constellation tells our tale,
Mapping a future where love prevails.
In the vastness, our spirits soar,
Finding home where we explore.

The universe hums a gentle tune,
As we dance beneath the moon.
Boundless skies, our canvas true,
Painting adventures, just me and you.

Through stardust trails and comet's flight,
We chase the dawn, embracing the light.
In this journey, forever we roam,
Nature and cosmos our loving home.

Cosmic Symphony of Togetherness

In the silence of endless night,
Galaxies swirl, a magnificent sight.
Together we play our notes so sweet,
In harmony, where heartbeats meet.

Each twang of chords, the stars reply,
A cosmic song where dreams can fly.
United in rhythm, finding our way,
A melody brightens the darkest day.

The universe dances, our spirits rise,
Underneath the vast and starry skies.
With every turn, our love ignites,
An everlasting flame that softly lights.

With waves of sound, we are entwined,
In the music of fate, our souls aligned.
Together, we weave a vibrant thread,
In every note, the words unsaid.

So let us soar on this cosmic breeze,
With every heartbeat, we seize the keys.
The symphony plays, our love unfurled,
Together, we write a story for the world.

Paths Illuminated by Kindred Light

In the twilight, we find our grace,
With kindred spirits, we embrace.
Each path illuminated, hearts so bright,
Guiding each other through the night.

Step by step, we share our dreams,
In the glow of laughter, hope redeems.
Hand in hand, we make our stride,
Facing the future with love as our guide.

Together we wander, side by side,
With every heartbeat, we abide.
In the warmth of our shared delight,
The world shines back, painted with light.

Through valleys deep and mountains high,
With our kindred light, we'll always try.
With every shadow that may appear,
Together, we conquer every fear.

So let our spirits blaze like fire,
In this journey, we'll never tire.
Paths illuminated, forever we roam,
In love's embrace, we find our home.

Orbiting Hearts Under Moonlit Skies

Beneath the moon's enchanting glow,
Our hearts collide in a gentle flow.
With every whisper, the night unfolds,
A love story timeless, softly told.

Orbiting dreams like stars in flight,
We dance together in this soft light.
Twisting and turning, a graceful spin,
Finding our balance within and within.

The cool breeze carries secrets shared,
In this moment, we are both unpaired.
Joy fills the air, our spirits soar,
Under moonlit skies, we want for nothing more.

With every heartbeat, our rhythm sings,
Lost in the wonder that love can bring.
Hand in hand, we drift with ease,
In this cosmic waltz, we find our peace.

So let us revel in this night divine,
Two souls intertwined, your heart with mine.
Under the moon, we shall forever stay,
Orbiting love in a celestial way.

Gravitational Pulls

In the dance of stars we meet,
A force unseen, yet so complete.
Underneath the cosmic swirl,
Our hearts align, a gentle whirl.

Tides pull softly at the shore,
Echoes of a love we store.
Waves of time unfold their grace,
In every glance, a warm embrace.

Celestial bodies all collide,
In this vast space, we do not hide.
With every orbit, every turn,
Our souls ignite, our passions burn.

In the shadows of the night,
Stars ignite, a brilliant light.
Through the void, we journey far,
Together we are, a shining star.

Gravity pulls, it binds us tight,
In this love, we take our flight.
No distance great can pull apart,
For love is the force within the heart.

Lightwaves of Likeness

Radiant beams in twilight glow,
Reflect the warmth that we both know.
In every flicker, echoes play,
A world united, come what may.

Waves of laughter, ripples wide,
In harmony, we shall abide.
From dawn to dusk, the colors blend,
In every moment, love transcends.

Phantom whispers in the air,
Moments shared, a tender care.
With every heartbeat, time suspends,
In lightwaves' caress, our love bends.

Illuminated, side by side,
In this brilliance, we confide.
A spectrum bright, a vibrant thread,
In the canvas of life, love is spread.

So let us dance through shadows cast,
In this bond, forever vast.
Hand in hand, through every test,
In lightwaves of likeness, we are blessed.

Cosmic Togetherness

Galaxies spin with grace and flair,
In this universe, I feel you near.
Bound by stardust, woven fine,
In cosmic togetherness, you are mine.

Nebulas swirl in vibrant hues,
A tapestry of hope ensues.
With every heartbeat, every sigh,
The stars' secrets soar and fly.

In the silence of the night sky,
Our spirits merge, we do not shy.
A unity that knows no end,
In every moment, love we send.

Beyond the planets, far and wide,
Together always, we do abide.
In orbits tight, we lose our fears,
With every glance, through endless years.

So let the cosmos hardly sleep,
In this bond, a love so deep.
As constellations draw their lines,
In cosmic togetherness, our love shines.

Twilight Bonds

As the sun sets, shadows play,
In twilight's hush, we softly sway.
Holding hands in softest light,
Our spirits blend, hearts taking flight.

Colors meld in whispered tones,
In the stillness, love intones.
Embracing dusk with open eyes,
In twilight bonds, no goodbyes.

Echoes linger in the night,
With every star, our dreams ignite.
In the twilight's gentle haze,
Our love brightens the darkest days.

With every breeze, a secret shared,
Moments cherished, hearts laid bare.
Twilight calls with a tender tune,
In this embrace, we are immune.

So let us wander hand in hand,
In twilight's shades, we take a stand.
For in this realm of softest light,
Our bonds grow strong, our hearts take flight.

Interstellar Touch

In the vastness of night, stars gleam,
Whispers of cosmos, a celestial dream.
Fingers of light trace our hopes,
Uniting our hearts, on stardust slopes.

Galaxies swirl in a dance so grand,
With every pulse, we reach for hand.
Each twinkle a promise, a love so true,
Interstellar touch, guiding me to you.

Nebulas breathe in colors bright,
Drawing us closer in silvery light.
Infinite wonders, we venture far,
Together, we shine like the brightest star.

Across the void, our spirits soar,
In the silent echoes, we explore more.
Time bends and stretches, lost in space,
In interstellar touch, we find our place.

Together in dreams, through night we glide,
The universe opens, with arms spread wide.
In the cosmic embrace, we shall forever cling,
Our hearts beat wildly, like the stars they sing.

Luminescent Bonds

Glimmers of hope in the midnight sky,
A tapestry woven where shadows lie.
Each star a whisper, a tale untold,
In luminescent bonds, our love unfolds.

Connected by light, we fear no dark,
In this vast universe, we find our spark.
Holding each other through celestial tides,
In luminescent bonds, our spirit abides.

As comets blaze through the velvet night,
We chase the dreams that shine so bright.
In the silence, our hearts are free,
Luminescent bonds, just you and me.

With every heartbeat, we intertwine,
Crafting a story, uniquely divine.
Through constellations, our pathway's traced,
In luminous paths, our love embraced.

Among the stars, we make our stand,
In the realm of light, hand in hand.
Forever we glide through the heavens high,
In luminescent bonds, we touch the sky.

Cosmic Reflections

Beneath the moonlight, shadows dance,
In cosmic reflections, we take our chance.
Mirrored in starlight, our souls align,
Timeless echoes, in the night, we shine.

Galactic waters, deep and vast,
Reflections of futures and echoes of past.
With every glimmer, a story we weave,
In cosmic reflections, we dare to believe.

Each drop of stardust, instills our dreams,
In the silence of space, nothing's as it seems.
Together we wander, with hope in sight,
In cosmic reflections, we embrace the light.

Whispers of time paint our fate,
As constellations guide us to the gate.
In the vastness, our spirits soar,
Through cosmic reflections, love is the core.

With each passing moment, the universe grows,
In the dance of infinity, our love flows.
Hand in hand, we traverse the night,
In cosmic reflections, our hearts unite.

Astral Ties that Bind

In the silence of stars, our paths entwine,
Astral ties that bind, a love divine.
With every heartbeat, the universe sings,
Connected forever, to the love that brings.

Orbiting dreams where the galaxies spin,
In the tapestry of time, we begin again.
Each flicker of light, a story conveyed,
In astral ties that bind, we are unafraid.

Through the void we travel, hand in hand,
Finding our place in a cosmic land.
With stardust whispers, we sketch our fate,
In astral ties that bind, it's never too late.

As meteor showers light the night,
Our wishes chase stars, pure and bright.
Together we journey, with love as our guide,
In astral ties that bind, forever side by side.

This dance of existence, so grand yet small,
We rise with the sun, and in twilight, we fall.
In the heart of the cosmos, destiny aligned,
In astral ties that bind, our souls are defined.

Cosmic Ties that Bind

In the vast expanse, we find our place,
Galaxies swirl, a celestial embrace.
Among the stars, our stories weave,
A tapestry bright, we believe.

Wonders of space, shared paths align,
Through the nebulae, your hand in mine.
Black holes whispered secrets of old,
In this universe, our hearts bold.

Gravity pulls, yet we soar high,
Invisible threads keep us nigh.
With each comet, our dreams take flight,
Together we shine, a radiant light.

Planets may drift, but our bond won't sway,
In the dance of time, we choose to stay.
Across the cosmos, our spirits roam,
In this great expanse, we've found our home.

Silhouettes of Shared Dreams

In the twilight glow, shadows draw near,
Silhouettes dance, whispering clear.
Dreams intertwined, like vines they grow,
In the night's embrace, our hopes glow.

Every heartbeat echoes through time,
In the quiet, our souls align.
With every breath, the world fades away,
In this stillness, we choose to stay.

Moments captured, like stars in a jar,
Together we wander, never too far.
Hand in hand, we chase the dawn,
In the light of day, our dreams are drawn.

As the sun sets, the canvas sprawls wide,
In the hues of dusk, we can't hide.
Silhouettes meld, forming one,
In this shared path, we've truly won.

Whispers Beneath the Night Sky

Under the canopy, stars softly gleam,
Whispers of night, a tender dream.
With every breeze, secrets unfold,
In the quiet dark, stories are told.

The moon watches over, a guardian bright,
Guiding our steps in the cool midnight.
Together we sit, hearts open wide,
In the silence, our souls collide.

Crickets sing softly, a peaceful tune,
While the world sleeps under silver moon.
In the constellations, find our fate,
Beneath this sky, it's never too late.

With every twinkle, our hopes ascend,
In the night's embrace, we find a friend.
Whispers of love in the quiet air,
Underneath stars, a bond so rare.

Celestial Embrace of Kindred Souls

In the cosmos vast, our spirits entwine,
Celestial connection, an arc divine.
Through the stardust, we wander free,
Kindred souls, just you and me.

Galaxies merge in a dance of fate,
In the universe wide, we celebrate.
With every heartbeat, our essence flows,
Embraced by the light, love only grows.

Through meteors bright, our laughter beams,
In the night air, fulfilled dreams.
As the heavens whisper, we find our goal,
In this embrace, we share our soul.

Planets may drift, yet we stand strong,
In this endless space, it's where we belong.
Through cosmic storms, we break the mold,
Together forever, our story unfolds.

A Dance Among Stars

In the night where shadows play,
Twinkling lights begin to sway.
Galaxies swirl in graceful bliss,
A cosmic rhythm, a starlit kiss.

Nebulae blush in hues so bright,
Whispers carried on beams of light.
Planets spin in harmonious dance,
Creating a symphony of chance.

Through velvet skies, wanderers glide,
On trails where dreams and magic abide.
Each step echoes in stellar song,
As time passes, each moment long.

Comets streak with tails of fire,
Igniting hearts, fueling desire.
While constellations share their tales,
In quietude, the universe exhales.

Hand in hand with the dusk we roam,
Finding in space a place called home.
As dusk fades into dawn's embrace,
We spin among stars, time leaves no trace.

The Sky's Embrace

Beneath the vastness, hearts take flight,
Dreams glimmer softly in the night.
Clouds drift gently, shadows entwined,
In the sky's embrace, solace we find.

Stars whisper secrets, old as time,
In every twinkle, a perfect rhyme.
Moonlight weaves through the silent air,
Bringing comfort, a tender care.

The breeze carries laughter from afar,
Guiding wishes like shooting stars.
In the stillness, our hopes ascend,
Cradled in twilight, where love transcends.

Colors blend as daylight fades,
A painter's palette where joy cascades.
Nature sighs beneath the twilight glow,
In the sky's embrace, our spirits grow.

With every horizon, a promise shines,
Infinite wonders in tangled lines.
Together we bask, hearts interlace,
Finding serenity in the sky's embrace.

Starlit Conversations

Under the heavens, whispers ignite,
Softly we share our dreams tonight.
With starlight framing our every word,
In the silence, our souls are stirred.

Galactic tales unfold in the dark,
Each shimmering star a shining spark.
We speak in echoes of fireflies' glows,
Memories dancing where the night wind blows.

Cosmic whispers guide our hearts near,
In the stillness, we lose all fear.
While shadows mingle, we find our part,
Starlit conversations of the heart.

Planets aligned, our paths intertwine,
Sharing secrets that feel divine.
In silent moments, our laughter streams,
Beneath the cosmos, we chase our dreams.

With every twinkle, a bond grows strong,
In starlit encounters, we both belong.
Under the heavens, our spirits soar,
In starlit conversations, forevermore.

Cosmic Interludes

In the tapestry of night, we reflect,
Every star a whisper, every light perfect.
Galaxies spin, a dance in the dark,
As comets brush by with a fleeting spark.

In silence we find the universe's song,
Notes of the cosmos, where we belong.
Time stretches wide, a canvas so vast,
Moments suspended, memories held fast.

Celestial secrets twinkle and gleam,
Inviting us softly into a dream.
Cosmic interludes, magic in place,
Framing the sky with ethereal grace.

As stardust we wander through infinite skies,
Bound by the beauty that never dies.
Each heartbeat echoes through galaxies wide,
A dance of existence, a celestial ride.

With every star that fades comes rebirth,
In cosmic cycles, we find our worth.
Together we journey, hand in hand so true,
In cosmic interludes, just me and you.

Firmament of Feelings

In whispers soft, the night takes flight,
Emotions bloom beneath the light.
Stars listen close to every sigh,
Their glow reflects the heart's reply.

In shadows deep, our secrets lie,
A tapestry of dreams that fly.
Each heartbeat sings, a silent song,
Binding us where we belong.

The sky above, a canvas wide,
Where hopes and fears do softly glide.
In every twinkle, stories weave,
A world where we dare to believe.

With every tear and every laugh,
We sketch our path, we find our craft.
The firmament holds our tender schemes,
As we pursue our wildest dreams.

Dancing Among Stars

Beneath the moon's enchanting glow,
We sway to rhythms only we know.
Our laughter rings through the midnight air,
In this vast space, we dance with care.

Each step we take, the cosmos turns,
In every glance, our passion burns.
With starlit eyes, we spin and twirl,
Lost in a dream, our hearts unfurl.

Galaxies pulse in time with our beat,
We move as one, with grace so sweet.
The universe hums a soft refrain,
As we cradle joy - let go of pain.

Together we soar, like comets bright,
Painting the sky with trails of light.
In this celestial waltz, we'll stay,
Dancing among stars, come what may.

Radius of Togetherness

In circles drawn, our hearts align,
Creating bonds that brightly shine.
A radius vast, a haven clear,
Where love encircles, holding near.

With arms outstretched, we clasp so tight,
In unity, we find our light.
Each step we take, together bound,
In this embrace, true peace is found.

Through trials faced and laughter shared,
A circle forms, a strength declared.
In every heartbeat, trust ignites,
A haven built on shared delights.

Forever close, we tread this path,
In every moment, feeling the warmth.
Together we'll rise, never to stray,
In this radius, love leads the way.

Starry Connections

Across the night, we find our place,
In twinkling lights, a warm embrace.
With fingers stretched, we reach out wide,
In starry connections, we confide.

Every glance shared, a story told,
In echoes soft, our lives unfold.
Together bound, like constellations,
We weave a web of expectations.

From distant shores, our hearts align,
Through cosmic waves, our souls entwine.
With every spark, a hope ignites,
In this vast space, our love invites.

With every challenge, we will soar,
Embracing the strength in what we explore.
In starlit dreams, together we see,
The magic of what we can be.

Guiding Stars

In the velvet sky they gleam,
Silent markers of our dream.
A twinkle strong, a gentle light,
Leading us through the dark night.

Each constellation tells a tale,
Of ancient journeys, of the frail.
They spark the hope within our heart,
A guiding force from worlds apart.

The moon's soft glow, a compass true,
Whispering secrets known to few.
In their brilliance, we find our way,
Through starlit paths, we choose to stay.

Wanderers beneath their gaze,
Lost in wonder, in a daze.
With every wish upon their fire,
We chase our dreams, we reach higher.

So let us dance 'neath their bold light,
Embracing dreams in the quiet night.
For with each star, a hope anew,
Guiding us to what we pursue.

Journeying Alongside

With every step, the path unfolds,
Together through the tales retold.
Your hand in mine, we face the tide,
Journeying through the world, side by side.

In whispered winds, we find our song,
A melody where we belong.
Through valleys deep and mountains high,
Our spirits soar, we learn to fly.

Every sunset paints the sky,
With hues of dreams that never die.
In laughter shared, in tears we shed,
We weave our lives, our pathways spread.

Together facing every storm,
In each embrace, we feel the warm.
A bond that's forged through time and trust,
In every journey, it is a must.

So here's to us, to roads ahead,
In every word, the love we've spread.
With courage high, we'll rise and strive,
Journeying onward, truly alive.

Celestial Whispers

In the hush of night, they speak,
Softly, tender, never weak.
A message carried on the breeze,
Celestial whispers, aiming to please.

Stars murmur secrets of the past,
Guiding dreams, making moments last.
Through infinite space, they call our name,
Each twinkle, igniting a flame.

In every shadow, find the light,
As celestial whispers take their flight.
A cosmic dance beneath the skies,
Awakening hope, where silence lies.

So close your eyes and just believe,
In the magic that they weave.
With every heartbeat, hear their plea,
In celestial whispers, we are free.

The universe sings, a quiet tune,
Guided by the watchful moon.
Let your heart soar, your spirit fly,
In celestial whispers, we touch the sky.

Exploring the Night's Embrace

Underneath the starry dome,
We wander far, we find our home.
In night's embrace, the shadows play,
As mystery unfolds in silken sway.

The northern lights begin to shine,
A dance of colors, pure divine.
With every breath, the magic grows,
In the heart of night, enchantment flows.

The moonlight guides our every step,
In the stillness, secrets kept.
Through the woods, where echoes thrive,
Exploring wonders, feeling alive.

In the quiet, we hear the call,
Of night creatures, both big and small.
With heartbeats synced to nature's song,
In the night's embrace, we belong.

So let us wander, hand in hand,
Through twilight paths, across the land.
For in this journey, we'll discover,
The beauty of night, like no other.

Astral Affinities

Stars whisper secrets, deep in the night,
Galaxies weave tales, in shimmering light.
Luminous paths, where spirits collide,
Harmony lives, in the cosmos, our guide.

Celestial waltz, a dance of the spheres,
Echoing laughter, throughout the years.
In the stillness, our souls intertwine,
Bound by the magic, of a love so divine.

Waves of the universe, carry our dreams,
Infinite journeys, and delicate beams.
In the vastness, our voices resound,
A bond everlasting, in stardust we're found.

Through nebulous clouds, our hearts find their way,
Guided by hope, we embrace the new day.
With every heartbeat, we send out a prayer,
The cosmos in motion, its beauty to share.

Embers of starlight, ignited and bright,
Illuminate pathways, through darkness of night.
Celestial bond, forever we trust,
In astral affinities, rise we must.

Galactic Interconnections

Across the vast canvas, the stars intertwine,
Galactic threads binding, your spirit and mine.
Through time and dimension, our stories unite,
In the tapestry woven, of darkness and light.

Comets and planets, like memories roam,
Each echoing heartbeat, a whisper of home.
In the dance of the cosmos, we find our way,
Galactic connections, forever will stay.

Wonders of stardust, unite us as one,
Infinite journeys, begun with the sun.
Though distance may stretch, and time may appear,
In galaxies shimmering, I hold you near.

Mapping our dreams on the night sky's embrace,
In celestial wonders, we find our own place.
Fleeting yet endless, like light through the void,
Galactic interconnections, forever enjoyed.

Through dark matter whispers, our souls fly free,
Bound by the cosmos, for all eternity.
In this grand design, forever entwined,
Galactic interconnections, fate's tender bind.

Bonds Beyond Time

In the echoes of time, our hearts softly beat,
Moments transcending, where memories meet.
Threads woven finely, through ages and space,
Bonds beyond time, in love's warm embrace.

Through the whispers of history, we walk hand in hand,
Past echoes of laughter, on far distant land.
In every heartbeat, across epochs we weave,
An infinite journey, in which we believe.

With each passing moment, our spirits ignite,
Painting the heavens with colors so bright.
Through the sands of the past, our dreams intertwine,
In the fabric of ages, our souls brightly shine.

With memories etched in the stars far above,
We dance with the shadows, of passion and love.
Time is but a river, endlessly flows,
Bonds beyond time, as forever it grows.

In this wondrous tapestry, our lives intertwine,
With each thread of memory, our spirits align.
Through lifetimes together, we search, we roam,
Bonds beyond time, forever our home.

Celestial Fusion

In the depths of the night, where silence sings,
Celestial fusion, where magic takes wing.
Stars collide gently, in harmonious flow,
Illuminating hearts, with a radiant glow.

Nebulas swirl in a cosmic ballet,
Painting the heavens, in colors that play.
Galaxies drifting, in elegant grace,
In celestial fusion, we find a safe space.

As comets streak by, we dance in delight,
A constellation formed, in dark velvet night.
With every heartbeat, the universe sighs,
Celestial fusion, where love never dies.

Through timeless connections, our spirits take flight,
Embracing the wonder, of infinite light.
In the pulse of the cosmos, we whisper and weave,
A tapestry vibrant, in which we believe.

In the stillness, we gather, our souls intertwined,
The energy binding, no barriers can find.
In this endless dance, our essence is shown,
Celestial fusion, we are never alone.

Dance of the Radiant Hearts

In twilight's gentle embrace, we sway,
With whispers of love, night turns to day.
Each heartbeat echoes through the air,
Two souls entwined, a moment rare.

Beneath the stars, we find our way,
In this cosmic dance, we laugh and play.
Hands like fire, ignited bright,
Together we shine, our hearts alight.

With every twirl, the universe sings,
A melody of hope that joy brings.
As moonlight bathes our glowing skin,
In this radiant waltz, we begin.

Time stands still in this sacred space,
Every glance a cherished trace.
With every step, the world fades away,
In the dance of hearts, forever we stay.

Eternal rhythm, a true refrain,
In love's embrace, we feel no pain.
With every heartbeat, our spirits soar,
In the dance of the radiant, we yearn for more.

Cosmic Conversations in the Void

In the vastness where no light dares tread,
Whispers of galaxies, echoes of the dead.
Stars converse in silence, ageless and wise,
Their stories unfold, beneath darkened skies.

Constellations twinkle with secrets untold,
In the depths of the cosmos, mysteries unfold.
Time bends and stretches in this endless sea,
Each pulse of the universe, a call to be free.

Between the silence, hear the beats of fate,
Cosmic connections that wait, hesitate.
Voices from eons past travel through time,
A symphony of life in rhythm and rhyme.

In the void's embrace, we find our place,
With stars as our guides, a celestial grace.
Holding our breath in the great unknown,
We are but whispers, yet never alone.

Through cosmic currents, we drift and glide,
In this dance of eternity, we coincide.
Together we weave these threads of light,
In cosmic conversations, the void ignites.

Tapestry of Celestial Kinship

In the loom of the heavens, threads intertwine,
Creating a canvas, divine and fine.
Every star a stitch, every planet a hue,
In the tapestry of kinship, dreams come true.

Fingers like stardust weave stories of old,
Of journeys taken, of destinies bold.
A binding of souls through the galaxies wide,
A connection so deep, in the cosmos we ride.

Cosmic whispers dance through the fabric of space,
In the threads of our lives, we find our trace.
Bound by the love that the universe spins,
In this grand design, where all lives begin.

Across the expanse, we reach for each other,
In the embrace of the stars, like sister and brother.
Through trials and triumphs, we constantly grow,
In this tapestry woven, our spirits aglow.

Together we shine, hand in hand at the edge,
A promise of unity, a lifelong pledge.
In the fabric of existence, love is the thread,
In the tapestry of kinship, forever we're led.

Ties Woven by Starlight

Under the moon, where shadows play,
Threads of starlight light our way.
Each spark a memory, a bond so tight,
In the brilliance above, our hearts take flight.

Woven together through time and space,
In the celestial web, we find our place.
With whispers of love that never fade,
In the glow of the night, our dreams are laid.

Through storms of life, we stand as one,
Ties woven by starlight, never undone.
In the cosmic tapestry, we find our thread,
With every heartbeat, love is fed.

In this endless dance of luminous beams,
We cherish the bonds that unite our dreams.
With every star that twinkles above,
Our hearts are stitched tight, with threads of love.

As the universe expands, our spirits entwine,
In this vast cosmic play, like stars we shine.
Together we traverse the depths of night,
With ties woven by starlight, forever bright.

Star Paths of Familiarity

In dusk's embrace, we find our way,
Under the constellations' gentle sway,
Whispers of light beckon us near,
Together we traverse, without any fear.

Each twinkle a memory, softly spun,
A tapestry woven, two hearts as one.
Guiding us home through the night so vast,
Echoing stories of our shared past.

The soft glow of orbs, like laughter so bright,
Reminds us of moments, pure and light.
In the silence of night, our spirits entwine,
Navigating paths in the grand design.

We dance with the stars, a celestial waltz,
Each step we take, undoing our faults.
The universe watches, with eyes wide and clear,
As we write our story in the atmosphere.

Bound by the cosmos, our spirits roam,
In every heartbeat, we find our home.
Familiarity shines, like a beacon of trust,
In the endless expanse, it's love that we must.

Heartbeats that Span the Cosmos

In rhythm with the stars, our hearts align,
Echoes of love in a universe divine.
Each pulse a comet, blazing so bright,
Together we journey, igniting the night.

In cosmic ballet, our souls interlace,
Drifting among planets, we find our place.
The universe whispers, sweet melodies call,
Two heartbeats united, they never shall fall.

Through galaxies wide, we wander unchained,
With every heartbeat, the cosmos is gained.
In silence, we share a profound connection,
Love as our guide, a cosmic direction.

Stars hum our anthem, a celestial song,
In the fabric of time, we both belong.
With experiences vast, and dreams intertwined,
We navigate life, heartbeats aligned.

Together we soar on a starry spree,
Infinity whispered, just you and me.
In a dance of existence, we freely transcend,
Heartbeats eternal, the cosmos our friend.

A Sky Full of Shared Moments

Beneath the expanse where the skies unfold,
Lies a collection of stories, painted in gold.
Moments we cherish, like stars in the night,
Bringing us closer, igniting our light.

Floating on clouds, drift memories so sweet,
Every sunrise shared, a renewed heartbeat.
Through laughter and tears, in the twilight's glow,
A sky full of moments, ever we sow.

Each glimmering star holds a story untold,
Connecting our souls, more precious than gold.
In the canvas above, we sketch our dreams wide,
With bonds that are woven, no darkness can hide.

Nightfall brings whispers, secrets to share,
Under the canopy, free from all care.
In the silence, we find our brightest muse,
A sky full of moments, forever to choose.

Together we shine, like constellations aligned,
In the heart of the cosmos, our fates are entwined.
With each fleeting star, a moment we find,
A sky full of memories, forever designed.

Celestial Collisions of Kindred Spirits

In the vast cosmos, our souls intertwine,
A dance of collision, fate's grand design.
With every embrace, the stars realign,
Creating new worlds, your heart next to mine.

Galaxies blossom with our laughter's sweet sound,
In the stillness of night, our dreams are unbound.
Through cosmic encounters, our essence ignites,
Two kindred spirits, creating new lights.

Asteroids of sorrow, we gently deflect,
In the warmth of your presence, our love we protect.
With each twist and turn, our paths intertwine,
Celestial collisions, forever divine.

Together we journey through nebulas bright,
Our hearts an explosion, a beautiful sight.
Through the chaos of space, your hand I will hold,
Kindred spirits dancing, in warmth against cold.

In galaxies infinite, our story goes forth,
Harmonizing energy, positive worth.
Celestial collisions, where love is the key,
In the universe's arms, you're always with me.

Mapping Our Shared Universe

In the quiet night, we trace,
The paths of stars in endless space.
Galaxies spin their ancient tales,
Uniting hearts where wonder prevails.

Through blackened voids and cosmic dust,
We seek connections, build our trust.
Each twinkling light, a spark divine,
In this grand map, your hand in mine.

Nebulas paint the skies with grace,
Reflecting dreams in their embrace.
As constellations weave our fate,
We find our place, it's not too late.

With each new dawn, our journey's told,
In whispered secrets, brave and bold.
Galactic whispers in the night,
Guide us onward, hearts alight.

We chart the course, both near and far,
For in this universe, you are my star.
Together we roam the cosmic sea,
Mapping our love, just you and me.

Cosmic Kinship

In the vast ether, we collide,
Galactic kin, side by side.
With every pulse of starry glow,
Our spirits dance, together flow.

From meteor trails to moonlit beams,
We share the cosmos, living dreams.
With every breath, the universe sighs,
And in our bond, no goodbyes.

As comets streak through midnight skies,
We find our truth through love's replies.
In every echo, a promise made,
Across the heavens, never to fade.

In stellar gardens, our laughter grows,
Among the planets, love freely flows.
With cosmic kinship, bright and deep,
In galaxies shared, our hearts will leap.

Together we weave through time and space,
In this grand dance, we find our place.
Each heartbeat echoes, celestial song,
In the arms of stars, we both belong.

The Light That Binds

In the stillness of the night sky,
A radiant glow that draws our eye.
The light of stars, a guiding thread,
In darkness found, our fears we shed.

Waves of warmth, through shadows creep,
In this brilliance, our hearts leap.
Connected through an endless beam,
Together we shine, forever a dream.

Moments flicker like candle flames,
Each spark a story, none the same.
In the tapestry of time we weave,
The light that binds, we learn to believe.

Illuminated paths that intertwine,
Through every challenge, love does shine.
The universe hums a gentle tune,
In the cradle of stars, beneath the moon.

As we journey through this cosmic maze,
We'll cherish each other, through life's phase.
Underneath the gleaming night wind,
We are forever, the light that binds.

Star-Dusted Relationships

In twilight's arms, our laughter swells,
Where stardust lands, a tale it tells.
In every hug, in every glance,
The universe shrinks, a fleeting dance.

With cosmic dust, our hearts entwine,
Each precious moment, a love divine.
Through laughter shared and sorrows cried,
In star-dusted dreams, we confide.

As galaxies spin and time flows on,
Our bond, like stars, is never gone.
Each twinkle echoes stories heard,
In the silence, a whispered word.

Through black holes and nebulous skies,
Our friendship deepens, love defies.
In the vastness where we belong,
Star-dusted ties will make us strong.

So let's embrace this cosmic fate,
Together we'll journey, we won't wait.
With every stardust kiss, we find,
The beauty of love, forever intertwined.

The Web of Stars

In twilight's embrace, they begin to weave,
Threads of light dancing, each one a dream.
Whispers of the cosmos, a soft reprieve,
Connected together, more than they seem.

A tapestry glowing, tales old and new,
With each constellation, they share their glow.
Guided by stardust, a radiant cue,
In this vast expanse, their spirits flow.

Navigating silence, through time and space,
They bridge the distance, hearts always near.
Patterns of heartbeat, a gentle embrace,
In the quiet night, they'll persevere.

Among the celestial, their stories unfold,
Adventures of laughter, of love and pain.
Grounded in passion, together they hold,
A universe spun, where joy will remain.

Underneath twinkling lights, they often dream,
Every spark a whisper, a promise to keep.
In the web of stars, their spirits esteem,
A bond so eternal, in silence, they leap.

Radiant Relationships

In the garden of hearts, flowers bloom wide,
Colors of kindness, stitched in each seam.
Moments of laughter, where love can abide,
A fragrant connection, a shared sacred dream.

Through seasons of change, their roots intertwine,
Strengthening bonds as the years drift away.
Hands held together, cross valleys of time,
Each moment a treasure, they grow day by day.

With voices like music, they dance in the sun,
Shared stories echo in soft, loving tones.
Through trials and triumphs, two become one,
In this radiant union, a place they call home.

Facing the storms, they fear not the night,
With a flicker of trust, they chase shadows away.
In the warmth of their hearts, everything is right,
A beacon of hope in the light of the day.

In laughter and tears, their journey unfolds,
Hand in hand forward, they venture so bold.
With passion igniting, a love that won't fold,
A radiant relationship, a treasure to hold.

Constellated Souls

In the fabric of night, where darkness does sigh,
Lies a dance of souls, both humble and bright.
They twinkle like candles against the vast sky,
Each sharing a story, a glimmer of light.

Bound by the cosmos, they navigate space,
Tracing the patterns of fate's gentle hand.
With love as their compass, they find their place,
In this map of stars, together they stand.

Through galaxies wide, they ride on the wind,
Seeking the answers that silence may keep.
In unison traveling, where journeys begin,
A promise unbroken, as worlds softly weep.

Echoes of laughter flicker in time,
Each heartbeat a rhythm, a shared sweet refrain.
In the silence of dreams, their spirits will climb,
Constellated souls, through joy and through pain.

With hope like a beacon, they light up the shore,
Navigating oceans of timeless delight.
In the dance of existence, forever they'll soar,
Constellated souls, united through night.

Celestial Journeys Together

On starry horizons, two wanderers meet,
With eyes full of wonder, their hearts take flight.
Bound by a promise, where dreams softly greet,
They sail through the cosmos, igniting the night.

Through stardust and comets, they write their tale,
With laughter like raindrops within the warm breeze.
In the vastness of space, where mysteries pale,
They're crafting a journey, where love's sure to please.

As planets align in a beautiful dance,
They learn from each moment, like pearls from the sea.
With each step together, they seize every chance,
To unravel the wonders of all that can be.

Among the kaleidoscope of dreams they'll explore,
With the wisdom of ages, their spirits ignite.
In the warmth of their bond, they fear nevermore,
Celestial journeys, forever in flight.

Through celestial wonders, their souls intertwine,
With hearts open wide, they create what they seek.
In the realm of the stars, their spirits align,
Together forever, each moment unique.

Navigating Shared Skies

We sail through clouds of thoughts,
In sunsets painted gold,
Guided by the distant stars,
Our stories yet untold.

With every breeze that whispers,
We find our path anew,
In the tapestry of twilight,
Together, me and you.

The moonlight calls our names,
As shadows dance with grace,
United in this journey,
Through time and endless space.

In the silence of the night,
We share our hopes and dreams,
Navigating shared skies,
Nothing's as it seems.

So let the winds guide us,
Through storms both strong and wild,
In this vast expanse above,
We wander, free and wild.

Embracing the Night's Tapestry

As stars begin to twinkle,
In the fabric of the night,
We wrap ourselves in shadows,
Finding strength in hidden light.

The moon spills silver whispers,
On secrets deep and old,
While dreams weave through the darkness,
Like stories yet untold.

We dance upon the echoes,
Of whispers on the breeze,
Embracing night's soft cloak,
Drifting with such ease.

Underneath the sky's embrace,
We share a gentle sigh,
The tapestry of moments,
As constellations fly.

In this quiet realm of wonder,
Together we ignite,
The flames of sweet connection,
Embracing the night's light.

Echoes in the Cosmos

In the stillness of the night,
Echoes softly play,
Whispers of the universe,
Holding night at bay.

Across the vast expanse,
Stars twinkle in delight,
Painting dreams with stardust,
A cosmic serenade.

From galaxies unseen,
To comets racing by,
We reach for endless wonders,
Beneath this infinite sky.

With hearts aligned in rhythm,
We find our voices blend,
In echoes of the cosmos,
On which our souls depend.

These moments stretch like starlight,
Connecting one to all,
With every echo whispered,
We answer the night's call.

Stellar Souls Intertwined

In the dance of constellations,
Our paths forever crossed,
Two souls in endless motion,
In unity embossed.

Through the fabric of the night,
We weave our dreams anew,
Like threads within the cosmos,
Stellar souls, just us two.

With every star that's shining,
A promise softly glows,
Guiding us through darkness,
Where love's true magic flows.

Amidst the vastness echoing,
We share our laughter's sound,
In the tapestry of starlight,
Together we are bound.

So let the heavens witness,
This bond that won't unwind,
For we are but the stardust,
Stellar souls intertwined.

Patterns of Unity Amidst the Cosmos

Stars align in silent grace,
Their dance a cosmic embrace.
Galaxies spiral, weaving fate,
In unity, we resonate.

Celestial whispers, soft and clear,
Harmony echoing far and near.
Through the dark, our lights entwine,
In patterns vast, our souls combine.

Nebulae bloom, colors bright,
Each hue a story, a guiding light.
Forests of stars, forever spun,
In this tapestry, we are one.

Boundless skies, our canvas wide,
In the cosmos, dreams abide.
Together here, we find our song,
In this expanse, we all belong.

As the universe turns in time's embrace,
Patterns of unity, finding place.
Through the vastness, hand in hand,
In cosmic flows, together we stand.

Sparks of Light in the Dark

In the void where shadows play,
Small sparks of light begin to sway.
Flickers of hope, brave and true,
Guiding hearts to journeys new.

Whispers in the silent night,
Courage found in fragile light.
Each spark a beacon, fiercely bright,
Illuminating paths of right.

Through the darkness, souls ignite,
Chasing dreams with all their might.
Together, they rise, more than one,
A constellation, brightly spun.

With every challenge, shadows cast,
In unity, we'll hold steadfast.
Sparks of light, a radiant flare,
In the dark, we find our share.

In the tapestry of night so vast,
Our spirits shine, forever cast.
Through the dark, we soar and spark,
Together bright, we'll leave our mark.

Unseen Bridges Across the Universe

In silence built, the bridges stand,
Connecting hearts across the land.
Threads unseen, yet deeply felt,
In every bond, our spirits melt.

Across the stars, our whispers fly,
In longing glances, dreams comply.
Though miles apart, we join the dance,
In every moment, there's a chance.

Fleeting thoughts on cosmic waves,
Confirming love that always saves.
The universe conspires kind,
We find our way, two souls aligned.

Unseen bridges light our way,
In shared laughter, night and day.
Together we traverse the night,
Uniting worlds, hearts taking flight.

Through every dark and winding path,
We craft a love that will not pass.
Across the void, through space and time,
The unseen bridges, truly sublime.

Interstellar Alliances

Among the stars, we find our kin,
In cosmic bonds, we all begin.
Alliances forged in twilight's glow,
Together, we shall rise and flow.

Planets spin in perfect rhyme,
Our destinies entwined in time.
Through stellar fields, we sail the seas,
In harmony, with cosmic ease.

With every giggle, every tear,
Interstellar hearts bring us near.
By starlight's grace, we chase our dreams,
In unity, we weave our seams.

In nebulae, our hopes emerge,
With every heartbeat, we converge.
Galactic whispers, visions bright,
Together we shine, a wondrous light.

Allies forever, side by side,
In the universe, our spirits glide.
Through cosmic realms, we shall depart,
Interstellar dreams, one beating heart.

Light and Shadows of Togetherness

In the glow of twilight's grace,
We wander on this sacred space.
Hand in hand through dusk we stride,
In whispers soft, our hearts abide.

Beneath the stars, our hopes take flight,
Chasing dreams that dance in light.
We share our laughter, banish fears,
Through every joy and all the tears.

Like shadows cast by silver beams,
We build our world from woven dreams.
In every moment, side by side,
Our spirits bloom, our hearts collide.

Together we are strong and free,
In shadows deep, in light we see.
With every touch, our bond ignites,
In endless dusk, we share our nights.

In the cadence of gentle time,
Our laughter rings, a joyous chime.
Through every fight, we find the way,
In light and shadows, here we stay.

Dreams Linked by the Stars

Under a tapestry of night,
We share our dreams, our hopes take flight.
With every spark, our visions soar,
In cosmic dance, we seek for more.

The constellations whisper low,
Stories of where our hearts will go.
With every breath, we reach so far,
Chasing dreams linked by the star.

From distant worlds, our wishes blend,
In starlit skies, our souls transcend.
Together we weave a silken thread,
In every wish that's softly said.

The universe holds our secrets dear,
With every smile, we conquer fear.
In the gentle light our hopes will gleam,
As fate unfolds our shared dream.

Together we'll navigate the night,
Bound by dreams that feel so right.
With you, my heart forever stays,
In the glow of love's embrace.

Bonds that Shine in the Firmament

In the silent cosmos bright,
We forge our path beneath starlight.
A bond that shines through darkest days,
In laughter, love, and gentle ways.

With every heartbeat, we resist,
The pull of time, the fleeting mist.
Together, strong, we face the storm,
In every trial, our hearts are warm.

We ride the waves of fate's great sea,
Hand in hand, just you and me.
With whispered dreams, we chart the skies,
In shared belief, our spirits rise.

Like constellations joined above,
We mirror grace, we mirror love.
In every moment, we inspire,
In the firmament, we never tire.

Through every glance, our souls ignite,
In bonds that thrive, our worlds unite.
Together, always, we'll take flight,
In endless journeys, hearts alight.

Comets of Companionship

Across the heavens, swift we soar,
Like comets bright, we crave for more.
In fleeting paths, our spirits meet,
With every turn, our hearts repeat.

Together we blaze through midnight skies,
Chasing dreams that never die.
Our friendship glows, a guiding hand,
In this vast universe, we stand.

Through cosmic dust and starlit trails,
We weave our story, love prevails.
With laughter light, we light the way,
In companionship, come what may.

In every spark, new journeys call,
Together, we shall never fall.
With you beside me, I can see,
The universe is ours to be.

In harmony, our spirits fly,
Like comets blazing through the sky.
Forever bound, our hearts will thrum,
In endless joy, we shall become.

Printed in the USA
CPSIA information can be obtained
at www.ICGtesting.com
CBHW070345041224
18174CB00083B/75